HOME SERIES

HOME SERIES
FLOOR & WALL COVERINGS

BETA-PLUS

CONTENTS

P. 4-5

This bathroom of a country house designed by Bert Quadvlieg has a floor in German Muschelkalk (shell limestone) from Van Den Weghe, combined with cabochons and tiles in French Sarancolin marble.

P. 6

A fireplace by Van Den Bogaert in a home designed by architect Stéphane Boens.

FOREWORD

ymbolising charm, warmth and a cosy and comfortable atmosphere, the fireplace is often the central element of a living room, adding both aesthetic and practical value to an interior.

Floors and walls are also of great importance for the style of a house. Their size and obvious presence means that they have a major influence on the style and decoration of the home.

Contemporary, avant-garde, traditional, rustic... So many different styles, all indicating the decorative tastes of the residents and revealing their priorities: long-lasting, natural, authentic, antique or modern materials. The range of choices is enormous.

Whether they demonstrate the owners' fondness for the past or for more modern design, floors, walls and fireplaces are signature pieces in the home and provide the perfect finishing touch.

This book reveals the diversity of options and presents luxury materials to introduce style and panache to every interior.

P. 8
A bathroom by Bart De Beule.
Floor in enamelled Venetian
mosaic. Bath and washbasin
surrounds in Marron Emperador.
A project by Saillart.

P. 10-11
Large square slabs (50x50 cm)
in smoothed St Baudille,
supplied by Stone West,
increase the sense of space in
this room.

A METAMORPHOSIS

IN BLACK AND WHITE

Interior architect Martine Cammaert (C&C Design) completely transformed this historic castle to create a resolutely contemporary home.

Natural stone company Van Den Weghe managed the delicate installation of the floors and tiles.

This is a dramatic design with floors that are an important element of the interior. The floors in this castle are a definite feature and contribute to the distinctive look of this home.

P. 14-16
A pure white Italian Lasa marble combined with a grey Pietra Serena stone and a Belgian Noir de Mazy.

A different, warmer atmosphere in the breakfast area. Another colour palette here: a table in Brecchia Nouvelle with inlaid Crema Marfil, both with a smoothed finish. On the floor, tiles in aged Giallo Reale with cabochons and edging in Moroccan zeliges.

Detail of a floor in aged Giallo Reale.

THREE GENERATIONS

OF EXPERTISE

I n 1913, Jan Standaert, a talented sculptor, started a company that, almost a century and three generations later, has established an enviable reputation as a supplier of antique fireplaces, stucco and moulding.

The current manager of the family firm gained experience in England and in Carrara, the famous Italian marble town, where he learned many different methods for finishing natural stone and sculptural work.

Today the Standaert company has a permanent stock of several hundred unusual antique fireplaces. As well as Gothic fireplaces, the firm also offers authentic Louis XIV, XV and XVI fireplaces. All of the fireplaces are restored by skilled staff.

Standaert also produces modern fireplaces in French stone, using time-honoured traditional methods.

A decorative eighteenth-century Burgundy fireplace in a symmetrical style, typical of the Louis XIV period.

This authentic Louis XVI fireplace with typical stylistic elements comes from near Mâcon.

A Louis XIV fireplace in Burgundy marble with a lining in sawn red tiles.

A beautiful eighteenth-century Burgundy fireplace in pink marble.

A Louis XV fireplace in unusual marble from the Stinkal quarry (northern France).

A timeless Louis XIV fireplace with simple moulding.

A Flemish Gothic fireplace in Balegem stone.

A monumental Louis XIII fireplace with Renaissance-style accessories.

BETWEEN MINIMALISM

AND OPULENCE

F or over three decades, Philippe Van Den Weghe's natural stone company has combined an instinct for contemporary architectural trends with real expertise and a passion for the profession.

Van Den Weghe was a pioneer in the preparation of beautiful and unusual varieties of stone, such as Pietra Piasentina, Buxy, Corton and lava stone.

In this report, Van Den Weghe presents two recent projects that occupy a position between minimalism and opulence.

Used correctly, Basaltina lava stone creates a look of continuity and beautifully accentuates the streamlined style of interior architect Filip Van Bever.

This bathroom is in a Greek limestone.

A combination of Spanish Emperador Dark marble with edging and cabochons in Crema Marfil. A project by Themenos.

LOOKING FOR BEAUTIFUL GEMS

Van Den Bogaert Leon is known primarily for its large collection of period fireplaces of outstanding quality.

Customers from all over the world visit the company in search of beautiful gems, as they greatly value Van Den Bogaert Leon's professional approach. Every fireplace comes with a certificate of authenticity and is placed within a historic context.

This collection of old fireplaces is complemented by an exceptional stock of beautiful antique floors.

Key words for the company are boldness and modernity. The antique fireplaces can be perfectly integrated into a contemporary atmosphere.

A fireplace in Pompadour style (nineteenth century) in Turquin blue marble.

An exceptional seventeenth-century fireplace (Louis XIV).

An original period fireplace (Louis XIV) in Burgundy fossil marble.

Washbasin in Burgundy marble.

A chessboard design in two
types of Burgundy marble.

A UNIQUE PATINA

Within thirty years, the Deknock family company has grown to become a renowned dealer in old fireplaces and floors.

The impressive collection of limestone fireplaces from the seventeenth, eighteenth and nineteenth centuries is Deknock's great speciality. The faithful limestone replicas are made in the company's own workshops.

This report also features a wide selection of reclaimed floors, including old wooden plank floors and parquets, sumptuous Burgundy slabs, terracotta tiles and church flagstones.

These rooms are in aged oak throughout, including the floor, panelling, doors and radiator covers.

The beams are authentic. The panelling and floor are in reclaimed oak.

Two floors in aged oak and a toilet floor in terracotta tommettes.

A Louis-Philippe fireplace. Floor in aged oak.

A Louis XIV fireplace and a wooden floor in aged oak.

P. 34
A seventeenth-century Louis XIII
fireplace in limestone, combined
with an eighteenth-century oak
floor with an original patina.

Terracotta
parfeuilles on the
floor.

TRANSPARENCY, OPENNESS

AND GEOMETRY

This recent project by Pascal François is a fine example of this architectural firm's skill at creating a practical style of minimalism.

The design is an open living space with beautiful views of the garden, skylights and large windows to create extra light and add an interesting graphic dimension.

Modernity and functionality in a streamlined space.

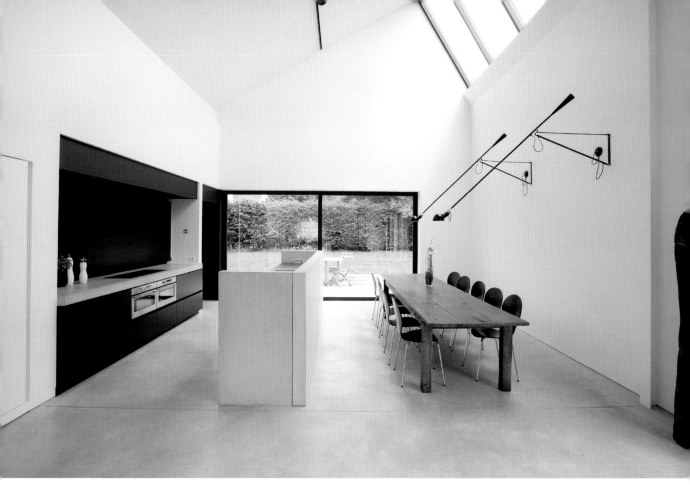

The floor in all of the rooms is cast in concrete with expansion joints to prevent cracks. The wall around the cooking area is in the same material.

DESIGNER FIREPLACES

F or over thirty years, the fireplaces of the De Puydt family firm have been key features in tasteful, contemporary interiors.

They combine the pleasure of beautiful design with the reliability of modern technology.

Their beautiful appearance makes these pieces an essential element of the decor.

A gas fireplace in a house designed by architect Marc Corbiau.

A gas fireplace was also chosen for this house, with its minimalist design.

ORNAMENTAL FIREPLACES

In this report, Antiek Amber, antiques and old construction materials, present four of the company's beautiful ornamental fireplaces.

A Louis XIII fireplace from the seventeenth century. Floor in Burgundy slabs.

This exceptionally beautiful Louis XV fireplace in Carrara marble, with its rich sculpture, comes from a Belgian castle.

This small, specially designed fireplace has been integrated into a new wall. An old oak floor with planks laid diagonally.

An elegant eighteenth-century French fireplace in beige natural stone.

650 YEARS OF HISTORY

The office with a desk and a chair by Ceccotti. The lamp is a design by Philippe Starck for Flos.
A dark finish for the original oak parquet.

T he clean and streamlined design of the rooms in this castle reveal nothing of the age of this sumptuous property, which shows traces of different periods, including the Middle Ages, neo-Gothic and neo-Classicism.

This historic interplay and the beautiful atmosphere of the site were Henrik Vermoortel's main motivations for creating a new future for the castle.

The pure white of the walls and furniture makes the floors stand out even more. The visitor's gaze is naturally drawn to the different finishes, including the strong and elegant contrast of the dark oak parquet in the office and the mosaic floors in the bathroom.

The clock tower has been transformed into a contemporary, monochrome bathroom. Floor and walls in Bisazza mosaic.

A SUBTLE MIX:

GREY BUXY AND PALE MASSANGIS

Interior architect Marc Stellamans was commissioned to create a design for this new property.

He selected a sober colour palette, including natural stone and floors in smoothed grey Buxy, furniture and units in tinted oak, chairs upholstered in dark fabrics and a staircase in natural oak.

The bathroom is in solid, pale Massangis, a French stone with a very warm appearance, here in a streamlined look.

Grey Buxy with a smoothed finish throughout the hallway and kitchen for a uniform look.

A serene, almost monastic atmosphere in the bathroom, with its solid Massangis clair stone.

THE RENOVATION

OF A HOLIDAY HOME

This report presents one of the projects of interior decorator Caroline Derycke: the renovation of a holiday bungalow to create a spacious family home.

The classic floor is combined here with subtle, trendy colours: a perfect harmony.

All floors and fireplaces from Van Den Bogaert Leon.

A palette of warm colours: dark walls painted in Sherwin Williams paints, a fireplace in yellow Burgundy stone from Van Den Bogaert, lined with old Boom tiles, fabric by Arte and Bruder, an old floor in church flagstones with cabochons in beige marble.

Two details of the reclaimed floor in the Smedenhuys. The beige cabochons have the same durability as the black church flagstones, but soften the look. On the wall, an old Moroccan door panel.

TRADITIONAL CRAFTSMANSHIP

T he sculptor Bruno Noël opened a traditional workshop in 1989. For twenty years, this enthusiastic expert has been creating his own projects, but he also produces customised furniture for kitchens and bathrooms, including solid washbasins and kitchen work surfaces and finishes for baths and showers.

Bruno Noël also creates magnificent fireplaces, carved by hand in French stone.

A simply designed fireplace in aged bluestone, polished to create a matte effect that harmonises with the old floor.

Wood and bluestone are combined in the bathroom. The shower floors are in solid stone (8cm thick). The circles have a textured, anti-slip finish.

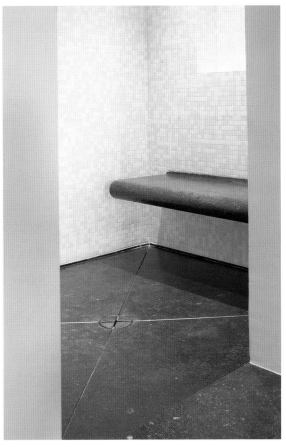

A solid washbasin and floor in bluestone.

A detail of the shower floor and bench in bluestone.

P. 58
The bathroom of a farmhouse restored by design consultancy Pentarch. The sober style of the farmhouse extends into the interior of the building. Bruno Noël created the oak unit and the washbasins in yellow Massangis clair.

A CARPET OF PEBBLES

This house was restored by architect Stéphane Boens and Dominique Desimpel.

Dominique Desimpel's passion for beautiful tiles and his sophisticated taste ensured an outstanding result.

The decision to create a "carpet" of pebbles in nearly all of the rooms of the house has resulted in a very distinctive look. This element is one of the interior's most striking decorative features.

P. 62-65
Dominique Desimpel laid a carpet of pebbles throughout the entire ground floor to create a soft, sensual atmosphere.

P. 66-67
In the bedrooms, terracotta tommettes for the floors.

WARMTH AND COSINESS

IN AN ENTRANCE HALL

Interior architect Laurence Sonck transformed this ground-floor apartment (300m^2) in collaboration with MGC (Eric Courtejoie).

The open rooms and the harmonised selection of materials and colours result in a simple look that still radiates warmth and cosiness.

P. 68-69

An oak parquet with a bleached finish. A gentle and modern look.

A HISTORIC HOUSE

WITH A CONTEMPORARY LOOK

Chris van Eldik and Wendy Jansen thoroughly renovated this sixteenth-century house, a refuge for sailors, to create a living and working space where old and new combine harmoniously.

This young couple own the Zon van Duurstede decoration company and the Job interieur line of furniture. They personally renovated this distinctive property to create a light and streamlined look where their creations are beautifully displayed and enter into a dialogue with a few selected works of art and antique pieces of furniture.

The subtle shades harmonise with the rustic pine floor.

The Job armchairs, upholstered with linen, are inspired by old models. The curtains are also in 100% linen. Lamps by Casadisagne.
An old portrait has pride of place on the mantelpiece. Wooden floors in bleached pine.

Oak plank floors in this sitting room.

A rather mysterious and sophisticated atmosphere in this room. A black tinted wooden floor.

Dark shades emphasise the dramatic character of the north-facing back room. Lime paints in muted shades to create an authentic aged look.

The first-floor dining room: floor in bluestone and greige walls. Job chairs around an old table.

A sisal carpet in the parents' bedroom. Fitted wardrobes. Linen curtains, Gwendolino bedclothes and a quilt by Society.

Bluestone, concrete and wood combine harmoniously in the bathroom. Walls in water-resistant paint.

A Hendrik armchair and a Casadisagne lamp. On the floor, a cowskin rug.

THE PATINA OF AGES PAST

A ndreas Van Apers started his company dealing in old construction materials in 1972.

Over time, he has gained a strong reputation, particularly for his large collection of antique fireplaces: unique examples from the fifteenth to the nineteenth century, in marble, limestone and wood. These unusual pieces are skilfully restored in the Van Apers workshops.

In recent years, particularly under the influence of son Joris Van Apers, the company has increasingly created a profile for itself with its complete interiors, in which antique construction materials and fireplaces are perfectly integrated.

This fireplace is lined with retro Boom bricks. A reclaimed oak floor.

The stairs are in old oak.

This door consists of wide planks in old oak. On the floor, old bluestone slabs, laid diagonally.

An antique oak floor.

P. 76 and above
These old Normandy terracotta tommettes are a perfect match for the limewashed walls and pure pigments.

The tommettes in the wine cellar and the kitchen date from the seventeenth century.

NATURE AND CONTEMPORARY ART

This house, built in the 1980s, is by architect Marc Corbiau. Obumex completely redesigned the interior a number of years ago, to satisfy the requirements of a family with teenage children.

The result: a look that is both timeless and modern.

P. 80-82
Carpets and curtains selected in harmony with the floors and furniture.
Modern art does not have solely a decorative function here, but is an essential element of the interior.

The kitchen's primary function is reduced to secondary importance here, as it serves as a passageway to a separate dining room. The suspended central block indicates the direction and draws the gaze to the frameless window that shows the nature surrounding this home.

Natural stone and an oak floor for the kitchen.

P. 84
The use of authentic Italian painting
techniques on the walls, the light
filtering through the wooden blinds and
the exciting pastel shades of the chairs
and the sofa create a timeless look.

THE TRANSFORMATION

OF A FARMHOUSE

T he exclusive construction company Tradiplan coordinated the renovation work for this modest farmhouse, creating a charming family home with generous proportions.

The sophisticated country style is primarily the result of the use of top-quality reclaimed construction materials: antique marbles, terracotta and old teak in combination with period furniture and modern touches.

Two old varieties of marble are combined in a chessboard design, with a small format in the hall and much larger in the dining room (see p. 88).

The wooden floors and skirting boards are in reclaimed teak.
The decorative fireplace and fitted units are in reclaimed pine.

In the kitchen, the old terracotta floor harmonises with the oak units and stone surfaces. The walls are tiled in old Dutch witjes.

RESPECT

FOR THE ARCHITECTURAL PAST

T his house, built in the 1990s, was originally designed as a loft with one large room.

Groep Moris recently completely restored the house in the company's typical style, with great respect for our rich architectural past and using authentic, timeworn materials, simply integrated into a timelessly classic interior.

The metamorphosis added an elegant panache to this home.

The kitchen work surface is in matte white Carrara marble. Groep Moris created the cooker, with its oven, microwave and ceramic hob. Old terracotta tommettes on the floor.

P. 90 and above
Old bluestone slabs on the floor. A ceiling in reclaimed oak and a wrought-iron gate, also supplied by Groep Moris. Stairs in old oak.

P. 92-93
This bathroom has a taupe sisal carpet. Bath surround in white Carrara marble.

A CREATIVE SYMBIOSIS

OF PAST AND PRESENT

T he company Architectural Antiques Theo Evers was founded out of a passion for historic building materials and a desire to conserve these pieces of construction heritage. This Dutch company has become one of the most respected suppliers of old building materials in Germany and the Benelux countries.

Theo and Ruth Evers, dealers in antique construction materials, form a unique pair. The key to their success is their personalised advice and wide selection.

Theo Evers' fireplaces, floors and decorative objects show a creative symbiosis of past and present, with a great respect for history.

A PASSION

FOR HISTORIC WOODEN FLOORS

Filip Redant is an antiques dealer and restorer with a particular passion for historic wooden floors.

The workshops of Passe Partout/Historic Wooden Floors painstakingly restore beautiful antique floors. This Mechelen company also specialises in installing reclaimed eighteenth-century oak floors.

In this report, Filip Redant presents a number of examples of his company's expertise.

This 17th-century oak floor is in three strips, separated by long cross planks. These suggest underlying wooden joists, which are in fact absent, as the floor has a screed base with underfloor heating. This look is, however, in keeping with historic examples.
The floor still has the original patina with traces of hand-sawing. The surface of the wood has a simple soap finish to retain its natural appearance.

A mid-nineteenth-century Hungarian point with original patina.

A 19th-century panel design with panels filled in with diagonal planks (with a mitre-cut edging section). The panels are arranged alternately to produce the distinctive pattern. The wood dates from around 1820 and was restored and treated in the company workshop. Passe Partout planed the surface, then sanded it down after installation, before finishing it with beeswax.

An eighteenth-century Versailles and Chantilly panel with the original patina, including visible saw marks and hand finish.

The Passe Partout/Historic Wooden Floors gallery displays several examples of antique parquet.

Marquetry in all kinds of different geometric designs.

P. 98
The star at the front of the photograph is a Passe Partout design in 19th-century style, in keeping with the surrounding parquet. This star is 180cm in diameter and made up of 1050 separate pieces. A typical period element here is the use of walnut wood as an accent of colour. The furniture and pottery also date from the nineteenth century.

ECCENTRIC AND ECLECTIC

The client who commissioned the design project for this loft is a flamboyant French collector of antiques and art: eccentric and eclectic.

An old, dilapidated warehouse in the city centre was opened up by the demolition of some of the buildings, allowing extra light into the lofts behind. The client lives in a loft on the ground floor and his teenage daughters live in another loft upstairs.

Stephanie Laporte opted for a sober, contemporary basis, finished with a sumptuous mix of antiques, art and unusual objects.

This seemed like an impossible assignment, with an almost impossible client, but resulted in a unique project that will have an influence on other projects that are yet to be developed.

The central space with its atrium and glass ceiling is furnished with classic pieces.

The guest room with its dressing room and a beautiful view of the central space, which is full of antiques.

Way through to the master bedroom.

The bedroom in the ground-floor loft. A dark-tinted parquet floor with panelling and bedside tables in dark-tinted wood. A lighting niche has been created in the wall behind the bed.
The sliding window is fully integrated into the terrace.

The bathroom in the ground-floor loft with its combination of dark parquet, dark-tinted wood and Moroccan zelliges. The central unit connects the bedroom and bathroom. The shower is finished in black zelliges.

A custom-built unit in Corian in the guest bathroom.

Concrete and grey marble are combined with white furniture in the teenagers' bathroom.

An illuminated ceiling. The walls here are decorated with classically inspired wallpaper. The washbasin is finished with Moroccan zelliges.

P. 104-105
The loft on the first floor with a painting of a view of New York in the foreground. Entrance hall with cloakroom, toilet and a freestanding wash unit in black mosaic.

IN HARMONY

WITH THE NATURAL LANDSCAPE

T he rural surroundings of this property formed the basis of this construction concept.

Hans Verstuyft Architects gave a contemporary interpretation to the classic, rustic atmosphere in their design for this modern home, in harmony with its setting.

The design was based upon a traditional house structure, as specified by the local authorities.

Orientation, view, light and privacy all played a part in determining the position and size of the windows and doors.

Contemporary furniture and pale wood and natural stone for the floors provide the finishing touch in this modern interior.

The long natural-stone surface in the living room serves as a bench. Large-format floor tiles in a concrete look reinforce the contemporary atmosphere.

The custom-built kitchen is suitable both as a workspace and as a dining area for receiving guests. On the floor, stone tiles.

The oak floor extends to the staircase, which has a simple plaster finish, maintaining the sober and basic look.

A SPECIALIST IN FIREPLACES

AND OLD FLOORS

In a little over three decades, the family firm Deknock has expanded to become one of the leading wholesalers and retailers of antique construction materials in West Flanders.

Deknock's main speciality is the company's large collection of limestone fireplaces from the 17th, 18th and 19th centuries. In addition to these antique pieces, Deknock make faithful limestone reproductions in the company workshops.

The company also offers a wide range of reclaimed floors, including wooden floors and parquets that are centuries old, magnificent Burgundy slabs, terracotta tiles and church flagstones.

A floor in old church flagstones with cabochons in white Carrara marble.

A design by Francis Van Damme, created by Deknock in old Boom klompje bricks.

Kitchen units designed and created by Francis Van Damme.
Floor in antique lava stone.

An early-18th-century Louis XIV fireplace in limestone with antique accessories and hearth plate.

An oak-plank floor with an aged, grey finish.

A late-18th/early-19th-century antique fireplace in Belgian St. Anna marble, lined with Boom bricks. An old hearth plate, grate and fireguard.

P. 112
Deknock supplied this old Carrara and St. Anna marble, arranged in a chessboard design. The oak staircase was also built by Deknock.

On the left, a work surface in Belgian red marble, made by Deknock.
Right, a surface in bluestone, with a smoothed finish and a chiselled edge, also by Deknock.

The floor in the toilet and the bathroom, an antique grey marble, was also supplied by Deknock.

HOME SERIES

Volume 9 : FLOOR & WALL COVERINGS

The reports in this book are selected from the Beta-Plus collection of home-design books: www.betaplus.com
They have been compiled in a special series by Le Figaro in French language: Ma Déco

Copyright © 2009 Beta-Plus Publishing / Le Figaro
Originally published in French language

PUBLISHER
Beta-Plus Publishing
Termuninck 3
B – 7850 Enghien
Belgium
www.betaplus.com
info@betaplus.com

PHOTOGRAPHY
Jo Pauwels

DESIGN
Polydem - Nathalie Binart

TRANSLATIONS
Laura Watkinson

ISBN: 9789089440402

Printed in China

P. 118-119
A project by architect Bernard De Clerck. A wooden floor in aged oak. Fitted cupboards by Francis Van Damme.

P. 120-121
A project by interior architect Esther Gutmer. On the floor, a coconut-fibre carpet.

P. 122-123
A wooden floor in solid, aged oak and Promemoria furniture (models: Wanda and Africa). The photographs in the background are by On Kawara. A project by 'Aksent.

P. 124-125
An interior by Obumex in a house designed by Froment-Delaunois. Floor in greige Buxy stone (Van Den Weghe). Stairs in aged oak.

P. 126-127
A project by Sphere Concepts.
An open gas fireplace with an oak surround. Leather chairs by Piet Boon. On the floor, tiles and cabochons in natural stone.